True Self / False Self

True Self / False Self

M. Basil Pennington

A Crossroad Book
The Crossroad Publishing Company
New York

The Crossroad Publishing Company
16 Penn Plaza – 481 Eighth Avenue, Suite 1550
New York, NY 10001

Printed in the United States of America

Library of Congress Card Number: 00-101127
ISBN 0-8245-1845-4 (alk. paper)

To Theresa Ee-Chooi
and
all those lay persons
who have dedicated their time and their labor
to open to their sisters and brothers
the contemplative dimension of life

We labor unceasingly
to preserve an imaginary existence
and neglect the real.

— BLAISE PASCAL

Contents

Welcome!

As I sat down at my computer to write this book I was profoundly aware of how central this concern is to each one of us humans on the journey: Just who am I? Who is my true self? Do I really identify with my true self? Or do I identify my false self as my true self? Is such a false identification the root of all the discontentedness I have experienced in my life? How can I uncover my false self — and get rid of it? Is this false self the self Jesus is speaking about when he tells his followers that we must die to self? How can I find my true self and know the wondrous joy of being truly myself?

These have been basic questions in my life. And I suspect at least at one time or another in the life of every reflective human being. By the grace of God and with the help of good teachers, I have found some answers. They may not be *the* answers or answers that work for everyone. I know that these answers can be expressed in many different ways. I know that there are different paths that can lead to living out these answers. And this I know. The answers that I have been led to and that I have sought to live have led me into a joy and happiness far beyond anything I ever dreamed existed. And they give me the constant promise of ever-fuller joy and fulfillment in my life as I continue on my journey.

My love for you should have been more than enough motive to write these pages and share these insights with you. But I must confess that I have finally sat down and written this book in response to a promise.

In the course of the past decades, whenever I was leading a Centering Prayer program, if there was sufficient time, I would speak about the fruits of Centering Prayer. I did this with a certain amount of diffidence. For if we practice Centering Prayer with an eye on the fruits we hope to get out of it, it is no longer really Centering Prayer. We are back centered on ourselves, wanting to get something for ourselves. The essence of Centering Prayer is that we center on God, that we give ourselves as fully and as purely as possible to God, not seeking anything for ourselves. We say in essence: I am all yours, Lord.

And yet we know that our God is so good that all

that God would have us do and be is to our own good. It is precisely in this that God finds glory. As Augustine of Hippo, who is considered one of the great fathers of the western Church, so beautifully said, "The glory of God is the person fully alive." "All things are yours and you are Christ's and Christ is God's," is the way St. Paul summed it up. While we do not want to go to Centering Prayer seeking something for ourselves, the Prayer does in fact produce very real fruits in our lives, fruits we want and need.

When I spoke about these fruits in the course of the Centering Prayer programs, the first one I usually spoke of is a transformation of consciousness. Then in order to put this in its fuller context I would speak of the evolution of human consciousness. And then I would bring it back to a very immediate and personal concern by speaking of the healing of memories.

This part of the program always excited considerable interest. I was often asked if I had written anything about this. My response was that I did not yet feel I was ready to write about it. I still feel I have not, by any means, totally encompassed the richness of these realities.

A few years ago I had the joy of bringing Centering Prayer to Malaysia. In the course of a very short time I was able to share the Prayer with over a thousand people, including many of the bishops and priests of that beautiful country. This opening was largely due to a remarkable woman of that country, the president of the International Catholic Press Association, Theresa Ee-Chooi. It was Theresa who extracted from me the promise that I would write a short book about the true and false self, about the transformation of consciousness and the evolution of human consciousness.

These are, in fact, very complex notions, open to many understandings and nuances, flowing from the various sciences, from theology, and from the rich and ancient teachings of many of the world's religious traditions. In my programs I gave a very simple presentation of these realities, a useful, practical view, a place from which to begin, and that is what I seek to present here. I am not saying this is just a beginners' presentation, but it is a place to begin to draw profit from these insights. Each reader, just as each participant at the programs, will get more or less from these presentations according to where each one is and what is her or his listening. And I am sure that the same reader, coming back to these pages after some time, will get a great deal more. For in fact the reader who returns is no longer the same reader with the same listening but in the ensuing time has grown and developed into a person with a new listening.

In the course of the Centering Prayer presentations, drawing from that most powerful and effective program, the Twelve Step Program, I often remind the participants that we must K.I.S.S.: Keep It Simple, Sweetheart! (Or is it: Keep It Simple, Stupid — I'll let us choose.) As I wrote this book I had to repeatedly remind myself: K.I.S.S. Maybe here it was: Keep It Simple, Smarty. There is so much more that can be said about every aspect of the self. And certainly about these key ideas of the formation and transformation of the false self and the evolution into the fullness of the true self with all the healing that that involves. But I think the participants of the Centering Prayer programs found my conferences exciting and helpful precisely because they were kept fairly simple and clear, so that the participants could immediately begin to use what they received as workable principles in their everyday lives. And it is precisely that practical utility that I do not want to lose in this written presentation. I want to say what essentially needs to be said with sufficient clarity but without, not only superfluity, but even without much of the rich complementarity that can be added. This richness can be left to another time after the essential has been grasped and has had an opportunity to become effectively operative in our lives. When dealing with such profound and rich reality the danger is for the speaker or writer to so overwhelm that she or he paralyzes. At the end of this volume I will offer a brief, selected reading list which you can use as you experience the desire to deepen or extend your knowledge of different aspects of this teaching. The volumes in the bibliography in their turn will give you further reading lists. If one wants to pursue it, here is the beginning of a lifetime project.

So in this volume I present basically two conferences: the transformation of consciousness and the evolution of human consciousness in the human family as a whole and in each of us as individuals. These are really just two ways of exploring the same reality. Dionysius the Pseudo-Areopagite, a fifth-century Syrian monk who has made an immense contribution to the development of mystical theology in the Christian community, used to speak of three kinds of contemplation: direct, oblique, and circular. In direct contemplation we plunge directly into the Divine. This is what we do in Centering Prayer. In oblique contemplation, we seek to see God or traces of God in the creation. Everything speaks of its Maker. In circular contemplation, we, as it were, circle around the Reality, perceiving first one aspect and then another, touching first on one attribute and then another, letting them all come together to give us an ever fuller apprehension. The exploration of the self that we are engaging in here is more of that circular type. But at any moment do not hesitate to let go and plunge in, if you are so drawn. My confrere Thomas Merton, Father Louis of Gethsemani, often said the easiest way to come to God is to enter into our own center and then pass through that center into the center of God. (I would like to take this opportunity to acknowledge my debt to this mentor as well as my debt to that other Fr. Thomas, Thomas Keating, the abbot emeritus of Spencer — to both of them I am immensely grateful.)

Truth is one. The paths to Truth and to a loving union with Truth are many. Just as hunger belongs to every human being but is satisfied with many different kinds of food, so the call to transcendence, to union with the Divine, is issued to each and every one of us humans, but there are many ways open for us to respond to it. We continue on an evolutionary course which Cardinal Newman so insightfully and reverently

17

described as the "development of doctrine." The early Church proclaimed: *lex orandi, lex credendi.* The way we pray as God's People is the way we truly believe — a truth so beautifully brought out in our own time and country by the leading Hispanic/Latino theologian, Roberto Goizueta. The reverse is equally true: *lex credendi, lex orandi.* As we truly believe so we pray. As dogma has developed so has our prayer. As soteriological and redemptive theology has been richly complemented in our times by a development in creation theology, so has our prayer become more and more a prayer or, if you will, a spirituality of being — redeemed being, and therefore a Spirit-filled being.

May spending time reflecting on the self in no wise lead to our becoming more self-centered. Augustine of Hippo, in undertaking the writing of his classic work *The Confessions,* prayed: *Noverim me ut noverim Te* — Lord, may I know myself in order that I might know you. This is a good attitude and prayer in undertaking a consideration of the self. Since we have been made in the very image of God, distorted and muddied though we may be, we are still one of the greatest means for getting to know something of the God who made us. In the more practical sphere, the better we know ourselves the better we can be in touch with our deepest and truest aspirations — which are longings to know God with that existential knowledge that comes about through a union of love — and the more effectively order our lives to that fulfillment.

Bernard of Clairvaux, the great spiritual master of the Cistercian tradition, in his basic teaching on love tells us there are four "degrees" of love. First, there is love of self. It can be good or bad, ordered or disordered. But a good self-love is an essential foundation. For how else can we love our neighbor as ourselves and how can we love God? Loving ourselves well, we come to love the God who made us and is so good to us, a love of gratitude, a second step in love. Getting to know this wonderfully good God who made us, and all else for us, we begin to love God in Godself, for God's sake and not just for our own sake — the third step in love. The final step comes when we come to love even ourselves for God's sake. Drawn up in an intense love of God, we can easily forget ourselves. But we find that God has an intense love for us. And, because we want to be united with God in all, one with God we love ourselves. Bernard says this level of love is rare in this life when we do not yet see God face to face. But as best we can, we do want to love ourselves for God's sake and to see our lives grow in the fruits of the Spirit, to be truly transformed, to evolve to the full potential of our God-given and God-like humanity.

In this spirit then, we give ourselves to these reflections on the self. May this reflection be truly beneficial in our lives.

M. BASIL PENNINGTON, OCSO

St. Joseph's Abbey, Spencer
Feast of St. Bernard, 1999

ONE

The Listening
That We Are

"That ain't the way I heard it!" How often has our report of something been greeted with such a statement? Or perhaps we ourselves have given voice to such a statement after we heard someone else's report. One of the arguments for the authenticity of the four Gospel accounts is precisely this. Each evangelist tells the story in his own way. The details of their accounts don't always jive. The words they put into Jesus' mouth are different. There are different emphases. One aspect or another is underlined. All this is completely consonant with our human experience.

Two bystanders witness an accident. Their stories are essentially the same, but they are different. And it is not just due to the fact that they are standing in different places. It is something within each that colors the witnesses' perception. Indeed, it might be in part just a question of color. One likes blue; it is her favorite color. And she does not like red. So her sympathies and her perception spontaneously favor the blue car. But it is probably more than just a matter of color. The listening that we are is a very complex thing. It is the fruit of a lifetime of experiences.

When I speak here of listening I am not restricting myself to the faculty of hearing. Our total being is a listening. Just as my ears listen for sound, so my eyes listen for color, my nose for scents, my mouth for tastes of all kinds. My whole body is sensitive to touch while my inner faculties listen for feelings, emotions, memories, ideas, and concepts. I am a listening, an openness to perception.

Let me display my erudition for just a moment and share with you a quote, the only Latin quote I re-member from Thomas Aquinas's monumental *Summa theologiae: Quiquid recipitur per modum recipientis recipitur.* Whatever is received is received according to the mode of the receiver.

I dare say, this display of erudition is being received by each reader in a different way. For some it is almost a complete blank. Latin just doesn't click with them. For some it might bring a moment of elation. That hard-earned Latin that has long lain dormant awakens to recognition. The feeling is good. The words make their special impact. But these folks will be few in number. Perhaps more will feel a certain anger. Such a vain display of erudition is experienced as belittling. And there may be attitudes evoked by the venerable Doctor of the Church: a nod toward venerated authority or a dismissal of this man who is perceived as bringing an intellectual sterility into Catholic theology. All these attitudes, perceptions, feelings are a part of the stuff that forms the listening that we are.

Our listening has, as it were, a certain shape. As perceptions come to us, whether they come through our ears or our eyes, through our mouth or our nose, or touch us in any other way, they pass across the shape of our listening. What fits within the parameters of that listening is perceived and can be taken cognizance of. What does not fit within those parameters will most likely be totally ignored or unperceived.

Though not necessarily so.

For persons who are rigid, who have very strongly established parameters, there is little chance for any perception beyond them. Such persons frequently harbor strong prejudices. And in these areas at least a certain amount of undue pride and arrogance. "I know all about that!" "I know what that kind of person is like!" There just is no room for any larger perception to come in to invite an expansion of the boundaries of consciousness that are set in concrete. They are concrete indeed and there is no suppleness about them at all.

On the other hand, persons who are more open, especially if they are aware that they are conditioned to be a certain listening, can with a sympathetic listening expand the set parameters of their listening.

Sad to say, I grew up in such a way that certain prejudices were bred into me. Of course this is true of all of us. And the prejudices that are instilled in us can be for the good or for bad. They can be more or less conscious. It may be a labor of a lifetime to get in touch with all our prejudices and free ourselves from the rigidity they induce in us so that we may move into true freedom. Among the prejudices that were bred into me were some of the worst sort, racial prejudices against Jews and Blacks. I heard repeatedly that Jews were this and Jews were that — and what I heard was not exactly complimentary. And much the same went for Blacks even though they were significantly absent from our neighborhood. Thanks be to God, I early became aware of these prejudices. Even better, I came to know some wonderful Jewish women and men and some Blacks, and the evilly defining lines were obliterated. I still perceive within me at times some fragmentary remnants of these early prejudices. And other prejudices are uncovered. These latter can be as insignificant and silly as a prejudice against Brussels sprouts and for asparagus or as challenging as Americanism.

There is no question here of praising or condemning the listening that each one of us is. The important thing is to recognize that we are a certain listening. There may or may not be a proportionate value to dedicating some time to discerning what led to establishing some of the parameters of our present listening. The insight might help us to soften so that the listening can be open to expansion in that area. But this is not always the best or most effective way to go about such change. In any case, before we can move in this direction we would have to come to realize that we are a certain listening. And that is the main insight I want to share here.

When I realize that I am a certain listening I am taking the first step in the journey toward embracing my true self. However far from — or near to (the glass is half full!) — the true self that the listening that I am is, it is a starting point. And having a starting

25

point gives me possibility and hope. I can move from here, leaving behind what is false. I can move ahead, becoming ever more true.

Another fruit flowing from the realization that I am a certain listening is the perception that my particular listening is necessarily partial. There are other listenings. And these can enrich me if I can add the richness of these other listenings to the listening that I am. Again, a cause for hope, a pathway to growth. This perception invites me to enter with enthusiasm into groups, committees, councils, and boards, knowing that each one of us has a particular and unique contribution to make to our collective insight and consciousness. This for me is exciting and one of the reasons why I am happy to live under the Rule of St. Benedict. This wise and holy legislator calls upon the abbot to summon all the brethren to council whenever anything of import is to be decided and to keep a small council of seniors for other affairs — to do everything with counsel.

We are each a listening. We can rejoice in our uniqueness. We can each make our unique contribution. And we can look forward to growth.

TWO

The Formation of the False Self

The listening that we are is the product of formative listening. It is the fruit of a lifetime, a project that is never really complete. In Centering Prayer and similar forms of contemplative prayer we do, indeed, seek to drop all our parameters or leave them behind and open ourselves completely to the transformative experience of God. This is the accomplishment of the pure of heart, and they do see God. But if we listen to the seers, the fullness of this experience is something rare for anyone still on the journey — rare and quickly passing. Quickly enough we are back to a more prosaic listening.

It is the same formative listening that produces the listening that we are that also forms in us a sense of self, which unfortunately leads to the creation of a false self when we identify with it.

The process begins already in the womb. Happily for the most part the womb is a perfect environment and the little person therein is quite content and well cared for. It is when the little one is ushered out from this idyllic world of around-the-clock care that she or he begins to experience need. Such basics as air, water, food, warmth, and comfort are craved. And whether the need is caused by hunger or a pin sticking in one's butt, the child has only one way of indicating its sense of need: a largely indeterminate cry. A very attentive and loving care-giver can begin to sense the message in the cry or soon enough determine it and attend to it. There are also the more subtle needs, which modern psychology has made us ever more aware of: the need to be touched, held, cuddled, spoken to, and sung to with gentle, reassuring sounds.

Whatever the level, the child's initial experience is one of need, of all sorts of things. And getting those things, having those things is the key to happiness and contentment, to a sense of security and well-being.

It does not take long for newborns to identify the source from which they can hope to obtain the things that are needed: the parents or the parent substitutes. The little one quickly identifies with this source, feels a relative contentment and security when the provider is

28

near at hand, confident that as the needs arise they will be met. A good relationship with this source becomes an instinctual motive. And this relationship opens the way for the parents to fulfill their educative role.

There is something that comes to play here that parents need to be aware of.

The parents' love is one of the most God-like things in creation. Together with God the parents have brought this little one into being. And like God's, their love is totally gratuitous. The little one has done absolutely nothing to merit it. It is such a beautiful thing, this wholly gratuitous love. There comes to my mind's eye the image of the husband of one of my nieces. Doug is a big man, tall and well built, an excellent basketball player, a real jock. I can remember vividly, one day shortly after his first daughter was born (they now have three), I came upon Doug, sitting in a chair, holding that little one in his great hand. His whole being was enraptured. There poured out from him, almost visibly, torrents of love. For me it was a wonderful image of the Divine Love. If a child always received this totally gratuitous, totally affirming love, that child would grow up to be one of the most beautiful persons this world has known.

Unfortunately what often happens is this. Parents,

conscious of their responsibility to educate their child, and perhaps, also, investing too much of themselves in the success of this project, feeling they themselves will be judged a success or failure in this regard, begin to trade off on their love for the child to get the child to perform in a certain way. They say to the child — sometimes actually in words but more often in their actions: "Mummy won't love you if you don't . . . eat your spinach, act like a little lady, be good to your sister, etc.," "Daddy won't love you if you don't . . . put your toys away, make a home run in little league, get a gold star at school, etc."

The message the little ones get through all of this is that they are not lovable in themselves. They are lovable only because of what they do. They have value, they have worth, they are lovable because they perform in an acceptable way.

This sense is reinforced by peers. Who is the popular child? At first it may be more the one who has certain things: the TV game, the sandbox, the bike, the swimming pool . . . whatever. Later, it will be more and more the one who can do certain things: the good ballplayer, the good dancer, the one who gets good marks in school, etc.

It does not take that long for the message to get

through to the developing persons. Their value depends on what they have, what they do, what others — especially significant providers, real or potential — think of them. Others see them this way. And they begin to see themselves this way. This is the construct of the false self. It is made up of what I have, what I do, and what others think of me.

For men in most developed societies it is the doing that takes predominance. How often, when a man introduces himself, does he add what he does: "I am Joe Jones; I am vice-president at Sperry's." "I am Phil Tam; I teach at the University." And if the new acquaintance does not add this attribute to his introduction, we will probably ask him fairly quickly: "What do you do?" This is one of the reasons why it is so difficult for many men to retire. For some it is seen to be a death knell and is in fact that. For forty years it has been: "I am Phil Tam, I teach at the University." Now suddenly it is: "I am Phil Tam...." Because the man has identified himself primarily with what he does, has made this the pivot of a false self, he has in retirement virtually ceased to exist. When he should be able to sit back and rest on his laurels, he is instead scrambling to refind himself, to create another false self.

Traditionally women did not get so taken up with

what they do. After all, what did they do but keep house and raise children — roles not held in great honor. So women more frequently emphasized what they had: their clothes, their jewels, their hair, their bodies.

However, times have changed. Today, Mary Jones might well be president of Sperry's. And Joe may be wearing earrings — along with other pieces of jewelry. For some years I was helping out at our monastery on Lantau Island, near Hong Kong. We subsidized a small ferry to make it possible for our guests and for ourselves to get to the mainland. The seaman first engaged gradually acquired more boats and sired a family. As time went on he handed on the work to his children, then his grandchildren and great-grandchildren. I used to watch the young lads when they first began to earn some money. At work they usually wore only the briefest of skivvies and some thongs. But as soon as they made some money they were sporting heavy gold necklaces and bracelets and ever-growing pieces of jade. They had to let everyone know that they now had it. I feared that they might fall overboard and drown from the sheer weight of their jewelry.

It is all part of this same construct, the false self, made up of what I have, what I do, what people think of me.

Stop for a moment. Ask yourself: How do I introduce myself? How do I want people to see me?...Is it made up of what I have, what I do?...Who do I say that I am?...to myself?...to others?...Who am I really?

For some this false self carries over into religion. There is some Person out there — we call that person God — and I do certain things to please God to get in return certain things that I want and need. It reduces religion and our relationship with God to a fairly clear and controlled affair. This is why some Catholics have had difficulty with the renewal. Before, they went to Mass on Sunday, didn't eat meat on Friday, and had it made with God. It was clear and simple. Now we can eat meat on Friday and missing Sunday Mass is no longer that black-and-white mortal sin. But we have to attend to things like social justice and care for the poor. How can we know we have it made with God? Maybe we have to establish a real personal relationship!

St. Paul tells us that Christ suffered the things he did in order that he might learn. In the three temptations of Christ we see him learning to say an emphatic no to the temptation to create a false self.

After forty days of intense fasting, Jesus was a very

hungry man. The tempter suggested that Jesus might establish himself by doing. It would be easy enough for the man who would later feed five thousand from five loaves to create a tempting meal for himself out of a few stones. But Jesus had a better food.

Then how about establishing himself by establishing himself in the estimation of others. Off to the high point of the temple they went. The courtyards were full of devout worshipers. Surely if he suddenly descended from on high and stood in their midst they would recognize him as the Messiah. But Jesus needed no such acclaim to know who he truly was.

Then how about having. What a sense of power, to have all the kingdoms of the world! That would certainly make him something. But this man was poor in spirit. He knew himself in his relation with God.

He would not find his identity in what he could do, in what others thought of him, in what he had. He was who he was before God and in God.

This is not the place where most people live. Rather we live in the domain of the false self. And it is not a very happy place to live. Oh, we can distract ourselves up to a point, acquiring ever more, doing ever more, being indispensable (even priests and monks try that), go, go, go. But those quiet moments do sneak up on us, and we are confronted with the fact that underneath it all we are still that poor little one who needs everything and has to bond with others to insure that we get what we need. And there are those even more challenging moments when we know and even sometimes are forced to experience that we can, all too easily, lose our ability to do, lose what we have, lose our standing with others. Oh, how the mighty ones have fallen, even presidential candidates and majority leaders. The appraisal of men and women is very fickle.

Yes, it is a fearful existence, living in this false self. And a perilous one in this competitive world in which we live. We must ever be defensive. There are always those who would be happy enough to take away what we have, no matter how hard we have worked to earn it, no matter how much we seem to deserve it.

And it is a lonely place. We must never let others get too close. They might just discover what we so fearfully know: that down beneath all that we have and all that we do is that little one who is all need and is ever trying to win the approbation of others in the hope that it might ultimately assure us that we are worth something.

It does not take long to construct our false self. We all too quickly, with a good bit of help even from those who love us most, come to identify ourselves with what we have and what we do and what others think of us. But then it becomes a lifetime project to increase this and protect it at any cost. Some can enjoy the challenge, at least in part, if they can keep the fears, the insecurity, the loneliness at bay. But most don't succeed awfully well. That is why we are not a very happy society. Rather we are a stressed lot, swallowing pills and visiting psychiatrists. And seeking a catharsis in wars that we turn into crusades at enormous cost to others.

Jesus said we must die to self. It is precisely this false self that he is talking about. This self which we construct and which in turn imprisons us and makes us serve it in varying degrees of misery. We want to escape the demands it places on us through our own superego and through a society that is wholly dedicated to fostering the values of the false self. But how can we escape? How can we die to the false self, if it is the only self we know? If we die to the false self and we do not know the true self, where are we?

THREE

Coming into the True Self

The best way to die to the false self is to enter into the practice of a pure prayer like the Centering Prayer.

Once we realize that we have bought into the construct of a false self and have come to identify ourselves, foolishly, with what we do, what we have, and what others think of us, we have made the first step toward freedom. The false self is certainly an enslaving master. Our whole life's energies have to be dedicated to the protection and fostering of this mirage of being. Not only that. It is the source of all our unhappiness. Every time you are unhappy, just ask yourself: Why am I unhappy? Is it not because I cannot do something I want to do; I do not have something I want to have; or am I concerned about what others will think? It will ultimately be one of these three. The false self is the domain of unhappiness. This is the insight of that Buddhist teaching which tells us to give up all desire.

With the realization of the folly to try, as it were, to create ourselves by our doing and having we can begin to take the first steps forward by laughing at ourselves each time we catch ourselves. Here we are trying to make something of ourselves by doing something or collecting something and, to make matters more ridiculous, telling others, making sure they know about it so that we will in some way live or be more in their judgment or imagination. Is Bill Gates any more of a person because he arrived at having a hundred billion dollars? Or Mrs. Marcos because she had three thousand pairs of shoes? Or for that matter, are they any happier? They have made their way into more peoples' thoughts and imagination, but that certainly did not increase in any way who they are as persons. If anything, these possessions may well have diminished them as the care of these things enslaved them more and more to the things they supposedly possessed but in actuality are possessed by.

If we can catch ourselves — Oh, there I go again, trying to make something of myself by this doing, doing, doing — and then laugh at ourselves, we will find a new freedom. I do not have to do to be; I am. To succumb to the advertising media that tells me I must have this car, this house, take this vacation, or even just use this cereal to be somebody — how can I allow myself to be so demeaned. But the media is clever, powerful, and effective and is supported by the sad reality that so many of our peers do in fact live by its imposed scale of values. It is not easy to begin to free ourselves from the construct of the false self, even when we come to realize that it is so phony. A good sense of humor, an ability to laugh at ourselves, again and again, is a great asset.

But where we effectively die to this false self is in the practice of a prayer like the Centering Prayer. After all, when we sit down to center, what are we doing? Essentially nothing. Unlike methods of meditation where we do something — watch our breath, use a mantra, etc. — in Centering Prayer we simply be. We use a prayer word, or a sacred word if you will, only in those moments when we realize we have again reverted to doing something: thinking about something, remembering something, feeling something.... Then we use our word to return to the simple state of being. Or perhaps, more accurately, it is not even being, but allowing God to be in us and express God's being in us, in our being. We are no longer doing anything: Let it be done unto me according to your Word.

Little chance here to build up a false sense of self by doing.

And what do people think of us as we sit there? Most would judge us to be at least a bit off the mark, wasting time, if not a bit crazy. And our false self readily joins with them in this appraisal. "Get up and get going! Do something! Why are you wasting your time? Isn't this all so stupid? Who are you trying to fool?" Etc.

There is a mixed blessing in the fact that many are coming to appreciate meditation, even the medical and psychiatric professions. For more and more people, meditation is becoming something worth doing: We get something out of it; it is an honorable, even wise thing to do. And thus it becomes vulnerable to being co-opted by the false self as something I do and something that can make me more in the estimation of others. The false self is ready to jump in anywhere it can find an opening.

And what do we have when we enter into Centering Payer? The last thing we are willing to give up is our own thoughts. Take everything else away from me, I know my own mind. The pernicious philosophy that has so formed our times, that of Descartes, has as its bottom line: I think, therefore I am. This is, of course, just the reverse of reality. I am and therefore I think, I dance, I play, I pray.... In pure prayer like Centering Prayer I give up even my thoughts. I hold on to nothing, to no thing, not even to no-thingness. I claim nothing. And I certainly do not seek to make something of myself for having something.

This is what I do as I enter into the prayer. And I have to do again and again during the prayer, by the use of my prayer word, for I find myself again and again reverting to my thoughts. It may be the things I am thinking about that are grabbing me: things I am doing or things that I have — again the fabric of the false self. Or maybe just the cleverness of my own thoughts or my ability to think. The false self is ready to grab on to anything in its gasping attempt to avoid annihilation. And so, in the practice of our prayer, save in those blissful moments when the Divine does indeed grasp us and bring us into our true selves in the Divine Self, we again and again gently use our word to leave all this phoniness behind. Even in this we have to take care that we do not turn the use of the word into a doing. It must simply be a letting go, a surrender to the Divine, who alone creates the true self.

To die to the false self is challenging indeed. All the

more challenging if we do not yet know our true self. If we die to the false self and do not know our true self, where are we?

But where is the true self?

As we said in the previous chapter, we begin our conscious journey with a sense of ourselves as a little bundle of need, needing everything. We have a sense of ourselves as an emptiness, a total need. This initial sense is an expression of what we have traditionally spoken of as original sin, a sense of the absence of God, of any caring loving relationship with the Divine Presence.

But what is the reality?

Some people think of the creation as though God made this thing and then tossed it out into space to let it fend for itself. By no means. All that is, is of God. At every moment the creation comes forth from the Eternal Creative Love. There is not a moment when the Divine Creative Energy is not fully present to the creation, for in such a moment all would simply cease to be. We are in some mysterious way a participation in the Divine Being, destined to be partakers in the Divine Life and Happiness.

So the reality is that when we come into being in the womb and come forth from the womb we are

42

not just some little bundle of absolute need. At the center and heart of our being is the Divine Creative Energy, an Energy that is Love, each moment bringing us forth in love. When we are willing to enter into pure prayer, willing to leave everything behind and go to the center, we open ourselves to the possibility of coming to experience this Divine Presence. True, it is totally within the Divine Discretion and Freedom to decide when and how the Loving God will reveal Godself to us. But the Lord has assured us: "Ask and you shall receive, seek and you shall find." It is with the confidence of faith and the appeal of love that we open ourselves at the center. And in ways beyond the meager limits of our rational faculties we come to know: know the Divine Presence, know ourselves in the Divine Creative Love, know everyone else, one with us, in that Creative Love.

Theologically we know by the Revelation that we come forth from God in Christ, the crown and center and immediate source of creation: "Through him all things came into being and apart from him nothing came to be. Whatever came to be in him, found life." And we return to God in Christ in that embrace of Love who is Holy Spirit. We cannot really comprehend or grasp this. We have to let the Revelation be;

we have to let ourselves be grasped by the Realities it expresses. Then we will know them in the love-knowledge that is beyond the rational intellect even illumined by faith. We are in the realm of the Wisdom that comes from the Spirit.

I cannot say anything more of this experience. It would all be stammering and stumbling. It is absolutely literally ineffable. I will fall back on the repeated words of St. Bernard (which used to annoy me when I was beginning on my own journey): "Those who have experienced this know what I am talking about. And those who have not had the experience, have the experience and then you will know."

Once we have had this experience, and even to some extent when we have embraced in faith the reality of this even though we have not yet experienced it, a "transformation" of consciousness takes place within us. The basic and abiding ("-tion") "form" of our consciousness is changed ("trans-"). I no longer identify with the concocted false self made up of what I do, what I have, and what others think of me. I now know that I am, existing within and ever flowing forth from the Divine Creative Energy of the I AM. Here is freedom, here is empowerment, here is life, here is love beyond all telling.

44

Certainly, once I know that I am ever embraced by the Divine Creative Love, loved by Love itself, by the Love that is the source of all that is, then I certainly will never again see myself created by what others think. If I am any longer concerned about what others think it is only because I want our relationship to exist in the domain of truth, to be what it truly is and not based on any phoniness.

In this experience of myself constantly and fully sourced by the Divine Source, I come to know, as Paul confidently proclaimed: "I can do all things in the One who strengthens me."

And I no longer need to grasp for things. I can have anything I want: "Ask and you shall receive." To quote again the holy Apostle: "All things are yours and you are Christ's and Christ is God's."

This is the domain of the true self — a place of wonderful freedom, joy, and peace. We begin to enter into the experience of that Christian koan: "I live, now not I, but Christ lives in me." Even as the Father begets the Son in an eternal total self-expression, so does the Creative Energy of the Godhead beget each one of us in Christ, the incarnate Son, the Head, the Firstborn of the creation.

We can go through many exercises, employ many

means to uncover the phoniness of our false self. We can in many different ways acquire glimpses of our true self. But it will be only in this freely given experience of the Divine at the center that we will come to truly know our true self and come to true freedom, with its love, its joy, its peace.

One of the great experiences of life is that first experience of being in love and being loved. Of course, our parents love us. They have to, or so it seems, and siblings, too. But the first time someone loves us for no other reason than that that person has in some way perceived our true beauty, our true lovableness, we float. We are ecstatic. For we have seen in the eyes of the lover something of our own true beauty. The only way we really see ourselves is when we see ourselves reflected back to us from the eyes of one who truly loves us. But the only one who can reflect back to us the fullness of our beauty is God, for we are made in the very image of God. This is what we experience when we come to experience God in the contemplative experience.

Even when we know our true selves, we still have to realize our social role in this world, in the human community, but we will be clear now that this is a role. It is not what makes us, but it is the way in which we collaborate with the Divine and our sisters and brothers in making this world and bringing it to its fullness. So what I do is important, very important, as a part of the Divine Creative Enterprise. It has an importance beyond anything I am able to grasp outside the experience of the Divine Creative Energy. What I have is precious insofar as it serves this purpose. Seen in this light its value is beyond anything I could otherwise ever imagine. And as I have already said, what others think of me is important for it is only to the extent that we can bring our relationships into the light of the truth that they can be true relationships and thus be the place where the reality of our union and communion in the Divine is realized and recognized and rejoiced.

But there is something more here. For in finding our true self in God we find everyone else in God. Indeed, we come to experience our true oneness with all in our common humanity and even more in our oneness in Christ the head of humanity. We are drawn to enter deeply into the mystery of God's love working in the life of each one of us. There is a union and a communion. We come to love our neighbors in truth as our very selves.

This experience of God and the perception of our

47

true self does not usually happen the first time we center — though God remains ever the master of the divine gifts and can give one this experience whenever and to whatever extent God wants. It may not happen the fiftieth time or the five-hundredth time. It will happen when God knows we are ready for it. Usually it is a gradual experience. We perceive as it were glimpses of the Divine in the activity of the Spirit, which produces in us the fruits of the Spirit: love, joy, peace, patience, kindness. . . . In our desire for more we should not fail to appreciate this. I have often had people say to me: I have been meditating for so many months or years and nothing is happening; I don't know if I am doing it right, or I don't know if I am meant for contemplative prayer, etc. After we talk a bit they begin to see that, yes, now they are basically more peaceful, happier, more patient. . . . And what certainly is a most precious fruit of the activity of the Spirit within: They have been faithful to their practice. What a tremendous grace it is to have the wisdom to set aside time regularly to respond to our Lord's invitation: "Come to me, all you who labor and are heavily burdened, and I will refresh you." They have become men and women of prayer. That is a tremendous fruit.

But the first time that the Lord does bring us into

that fullness of experience, which St. Bernard calls "the visit of the Word," our whole being says: "All the years of meditation were worth it, and even if this never happens again, it is worth it. The rest of my life I will center regularly." Indeed, if we miss a regular meditation time, we sort of fear that it was the time God was going to come, the Word was going to visit us. For if we continue to be faithful, these visits will continue until we sense a constant abiding Presence. And we know a joy that we had no idea could really exist this side of heaven.

When we perceive more and more clearly our true self in God, we are all but dazzled by the wonder of this image of God. But at the same time we are profoundly humbled. For we know that we were made in the image and likeness of God. But sin has come into our lives. While the image ever remains there, the likeness is badly scarred. And we know that, but for the grace of God, it could be wholly lost. This perception could mar if not shatter our happiness if, at the same time as we experience the Divine Creative Energy which is Love at work in us, we did not also perceive the Divine Redemptive Energy, that same Love, healing and making us whole. For the Love that God is, is something more than love. It is Mercy. "God's Mercy is above all God's works." Love perceives the good and responds to it. Mercy perceives the lack of good, which is what sin is, and makes us good so that we are wholly worthy to be embraced by the Divine Love.

A contemplative prayer like Centering Prayer is profoundly healing. We shall take a further look at this. But first let us take a look at this coming into the true self from another perspective, placing it in its universal context: the evolution of human consciousness.

FOUR

The Evolution of Human Consciousness

I am happy to see that the behaviorists of today who are exploring this question of the evolution of human consciousness are coming up with a basic hypothesis that fits in well with that of the great theologians of our Christian tradition, such as Thomas Aquinas, who in this depends on that great Byzantine Christian theologian St. John of Damascus.

Goodness is diffusive of itself, Aquinas would say. Speaking from our temporal outlook, we can say that "when" God decided to share the fullness of God's Life and Being and the abundance of the Divine Joy, God, a pure Spirit, reached out as far as possible and created the extreme opposite: pure matter. While these great saintly theologians were in touch with the immanent presence of the Divine Creative Energy in the creation, they could not know in concrete fact what we know today, thanks to the molecular sciences. We know now that what seems to be inert matter is in fact a sea of chaotic energy, bound and condensed, in some way contained and brought into order by an amazing interplay of forces. The book you hold in hand may seem quite inert and harmless, but if the energy within it was suddenly released without any control it could indeed bring this world to an end. Through the seething energy within, the Divine Creative Energy moved the creation along through fifty billion years (that seems the most common estimation coming from present-day science) preparing it for its crowning in the evolution of the rational being made in the very image and likeness of God.

What the sciences have not been able to tell us is where the original impulse came from, whether this universe which they study is the first or if it comes forth from the debris of a previous one, and so on. But where did it all begin? This we can know only from the One who began it, the Creator, who in the Divine Goodness has revealed this to us. Another gap, which not all scientists are willing to admit, is the leap into rationality. Again the Revelation tells us the story: It was God who formed the first humans, giving them a soul with the potential for sharing in the fullness of Divine Life.

We pick up the story of evolution at the point when the human first begins to function as a human. It is an era we know more by hypothesis than established data. We can call this first period, lost beyond history, the Alpha Period. Father Thomas Keating has called it the Uroboric Period, adopting the mythological nomenclature set forth by Ken Wilber. I would rather steer away from pagan mythologies and look at things from a perspective enlightened primarily by science and Revelation, while still remaining open to the insights of other creative minds.

In the very first stirrings of human consciousness, the Alpha Age, there could have been little perceptible to distinguish the human from the Australopithecines and the other prehumans from which they evolved, even though there was already present in the human spirit the whole potential for divinization. What glimmers of human consciousness that might have been seen would have been found in the areas of basics: the quest for survival through habitation, nutrition, and propagation. As with all the animal kingdom, survival was the key here.

But through the workings of the Divine Creative

Energies, the evolution pressed forward with the impetus of the human spirit within. As humans moved into what we might call the Beta Period (what Father Keating calls the typhonic, harking back to Typhon, that mythological creature who was half animal and half human), they became aware of their bodily selves and of their superiority to the rest of the animal kingdom. In the Genesis myth we hear of God bringing all the animals to Adam, and he gave each its name, thus signifying his dominion over them. And he realized that none of them was like unto himself. He was something more.

With this evolution the human was no longer concerned primarily with the barest necessities of survival but could look to a more humane and pleasurable existence, one served by the rest of creation, especially through the newly discovered command over fire and the ability to use animals. With light at their beck and call humans found more suitable habitation deep within caves, where they could wrap themselves in furs and enjoy charcoal-broiled steaks while the leaping flames brought to life the frescoes they had painted on their walls. It was still a period when human consciousness was centered in the body, this Beta Period, but it was an enriched life. Beyond survival, the human began to seek and enjoy some of the most primitive pleasures of human life.

For this Beta Period scientists begin to have more and more data on which to base their hypotheses. I will not attempt in this slim volume to present that data, neither here nor in regard to the other periods as we move along. My aim is to give the merest outline with some pertinent content to the extent that this is useful to us on our personal and communal journey, living out the evolution in our own lives and moving it forward for our human family. Those who wish to pursue the data more extensively can find many excellent scientific works as well as the offerings in the reading list at the end of this volume.

Through the Beta Period of evolution, the human was still constantly on the move, a hunter and forager, always in search of food. A new period dawned with the development of agriculture. And this had a profound effect on the evolving human. Some have postulated even a radical shift of consciousness. With agriculture we (for these are our ancestors) were able in some reasonable way to assure ourselves of food. But it was necessary to have control over a certain amount of land, with help to cultivate it and defend it. This brought in a whole new element of power. It was during this period that weaponry and war emerged. Some also see in this period a dramatic shift. Up to now, they would postulate, the woman, close to earth and the source of life as she brought forth new life, was the center and dominating force. But with this new development, it was the stronger male defender of the land who emerged in dominance. The woman stayed home, raised the children, cared for the crops.

Father Keating calls this the "Mythic-Membership Period," highlighting an important dimension of this stage of evolution. Living together in a more stable grouping, together bringing forth their subsistence, together defending their land with which they often sensed a deep bonding, humans now found identity in the group. The sense of oneself as an individual had not yet emerged. One belonged to the group and lived with and for the group in a very basic instinctual way. So we might call this the Gamma Period.

During this Gamma Period, as through the previous periods, the human brain was developing. From a small organ comparable to that of the serpentine brain (and still present in us in the form of the basal brain), this human organ continued to develop and grow. The human spirit had a more and more apt organ through which to operate.

With the full physiological development of the human brain we come into the Iota Period, where the individual, the "I," emerges from the group. With the potential now present of full rationality (thus Father Keating well names this the "Rational-Egoic" Period) we humans can now reflectively know ourselves and make freely determined choices, choices that can even be illumined by a divinely given Revelation.

It is within this Iota Period, which opened some three thousand years ago, earlier perhaps among some groupings, that we now find ourselves. Does it end here? By no means. On every side we sense the aspiration of the individual for communion, community, union. There is an enlightened desire to take full possession of the male and female within each one of us and to integrate them. We realize more and more the need for the speculative dimension of the rational intellect to be complemented by the intuitive, sapiential, contemplative dimension — the heart knowledge that takes us beyond. We strive toward the Tau Period, the era of community, integration, and transcendence.

All through the course of the evolution, as far back as historical records, mythology, and shared memory take us, there have been present to us seers, "see-ers," the ones who saw beyond the present era of human evolution and pointed to the beyond. There were the Rishis in India, Lao Tzu in China, Abraham, Moses, and the other prophets. Finally there is the Lord Jesus, the crowning of the human race, very God incarnate, who points us to our ultimate destiny: complete union and communion with God in Christ in the embrace of that Love who is Holy Spirit. This is something beyond advaita, something indicated to us in the revelation of the Divine Trinity, where One, who is absolutely one, is three, able to express themselves in the ecstatic joy of total self-expressing Love. This is the Omega Period, or better the Omega Point, where human evolution is truly consummated.

As I have said, we live within the Iota Period. It is a decisive time. We can move ahead to integration, transcendence, and consummation. Or we can fall back and seek our fulfillment in the quests of earlier periods: survival, pleasure, and power. We see the struggle all about us. We have seen it dramatically on the world scene. Hitler pushed the German people back from the rationality of our Iota consciousness to the mythic membership of the great Aryan race, to produce a power for conquest. In large part, the Japanese were still at the Gamma level of consciousness, seeing themselves all as children of the divine emperor, thus affording him, or more truly his generals, with a war machine. Did not President Reagan appeal to these more primitive levels of consciousness: An exaggerated Americanism had to prove we were the most powerful people in the world, made for pleasure (as we moved from the number-one creditor nation in the world to the number-one debtor nation) and secured by fantastic star-war technology that landed on the trash heap when he left office — very expensive trash that could have funded a raised standard of living for every person on this planet.

It is a time of choice. And each one of us can make a difference. Each one of us seeking transcendence through personal integration and meditation raises the whole. This is what Jesus was talking about when he spoke of us as leaven. Gandhi expressed it this way: If one percent of the people will meditate, we will have peace. This seems to have been achieved in South Africa thanks to the quiet but devoted efforts of a few persons with great vision. May it be preserved. At the same time, if many continue to pursue power, pleasure, and survival without a care for the evolution and integration of the human family, we will see the devastating chaos that is already plaguing many places in our world increase exponentially. Each of us has a choice to make.

We will be part of the problem or part of the solution. We can hardly stand still. The forces from within and from without work to drag us down, even as the forces for evolution and consummation are also powerfully present. Where sin abounds, grace abounds yet more. But each of us has the freedom to open ourselves to grace and transcendence through meditation/contemplation or to satisfy our appetites for pleasure and power. Let us now look at the individual a little more closely.

Summary

From pure matter to Divine Spirit

Alpha Period: dawning of human consciousness (uroboric)

Beta Period: bodily consciousness (typhonic)

Gamma Period: group consciousness (mythic-membership)

Iota Period: individual consciousness (rational-egoic)

Tau Period: transcendent consciousness
(integration, community)

Omega Point: unitive consciousness
(Cosmic Christ)

Readers who are uncomfortable with the theory of
evolution may prescind from that theory and still work
with the basic thrust of this chapter, namely, that there
are forces in us that seek to pull us down toward a more
animalistic way of acting even while we experience a
call to communion and transcendence. An individu-
alistic or nationalistic or ethnic quest for happiness
in power and security through dominance can only
lead to continuing destructive struggles. Our hope as
a human family lies in the acknowledgment that we
are one, meant to share this creation as a mutually
caring community.

FIVE

Healing of Memories

*Where there is healing Reality
there is the reality of healing.*

The journey of the human family, which we have just sketched out in a very summary but I hope useful way, is a journey which each one of us as individuals has to make on our own.

When we are in the womb and as we come forth, we are totally into survival. We need everything and even more the sense of security that comes from knowing that they will be provided. We have this, usually well enough, in the womb. As we come forth, we depend on others to provide.

As we continue to develop and grow, we come into what many call "the terrible twos." If there is anything you do not want a two-year-old to play with you had better get it far out of reach. It is a time of great discovery and extremely rapid development. And everything belongs to us for our exploration and pleasure. It is a wonderful time to be alive. A time of great pleasure.

We go on: four, five, six.... We come to know ourselves as part of a family. Now my father is the strongest man in the world, my mother the most beautiful. My big brother (or uncle) can beat up every other kid in the neighborhood. We are empowered by belonging to this particular group we call our family. Our family can and will provide for all our needs, will support us in every way, better than any one else can.

With this solid background we are now ready to step forward and be our own person, an "I." With the physical development of our brain and the cultivation of our mind we are able to begin to think things through and take responsibility for our actions. We have become rational and have decisions to make in regard to our lives.

We are now ready to begin to give ourselves as active contributing members of society, of the community, where we can find security, empowerment, and pleasure. I have been delighted to read in the newspaper, just in the last few weeks, of some young teenagers who have taken the initiative to start what are becoming extensive movements to better the lot of others in this world.

And young people are being called forth to take their role in evangelization. If they are themselves introduced into the fullness of our Christian heritage, this will include sharing those ways by which one can transcend the limitations of the rational intellect and enter into a healing and integrating union with the Divine. They will come to know, not only in catechism answers and creedal formulas but also in actual experience, their call to be one with Christ in God. The consummation of the journey with all its wonder is in sight: Christ, the Cosmic Christ, the Omega Point.

This is the journey we are all on, which we all have to make.

Unfortunately, none of us has made nor is making this journey unscathed. One of the great steps into maturity is accepting that our parents, like ourselves, are poor, weak, stupid sinners and that we have suffered a great deal under their care, no matter how loving they were and wanted to be. We can never thank them enough for the gift of life — something we perhaps appreciate more in this age of easy and frequent abortions. Nonetheless we have suffered from their heritage and that of all our forebears who went before them. And from all those about us, our great human family.

Good obstetricians are well aware today of some of the influences that can come to bear on a child in the womb. They will advise parents already at four or five months to begin to talk lovingly to the child in the womb, to sing to the child and pray with the child. So when the child comes forth the little one can hear a loving voice that is already a part of his or her experience which will ease the trauma of birth. Conversely, loud harsh shouts (of perhaps arguing parents), jarring sounds, and, even more so, shocks and knocks can terrify the little one. One might wonder, too, if the anti-child atmosphere of our age of birth control and abortion might not invade even the womb and infect the developing child.

Then comes birth. What an experience. All the more so when many of us were born. The newborn is forcefully expelled from the warm, totally providing, totally embracing comfort of the womb out into an alien world. For many of us, it was into the brilliant sterility of the delivery room, with its coldness and blinding lights. We were held upside down, whacked until we screamed, and then thrown into a bassinet and wheeled off to a room filled with twenty other screaming little ones. And left there untouched by human hands. Fortunately, today a wiser disposition prevails. The delivery room is warm and dimmed and filled with gentle music. As we come forth we are placed on our father's warm breast and hear his familiar voice. Then we are settled snuggly between our mother's breasts and hear again loving sounds that are familiar.

Nonetheless, even with all of these improvements, birth is still a traumatic experience. And the trauma goes on. While before, in the womb, everything we needed was automatically provided, now not even the most loving of parental care can provide for us in the same total, round-the-clock way. And often enough it is not just the pangs of hunger or gas or the uncomfortable dampness of a messy diaper that is the problem. A pin is sticking us or something seems so tight we are gasping for air. And all we can do is thrash about and cry, and sometimes we cannot manage even that. And tragically far worse can happen, from accidents where a child is dropped to the manifold horrors of child abuse.

Whatever the threatening experiences we undergo, they are all registered in us, the memory holding not only the experience but all the emotion that surrounds it. Tapes, as it were, memory tapes are encoded. And when one experience follows another, it has not only its own emotional impact, but it sets off the similar tapes in the memory with all their emotional content. All of these threatening experiences with their emotional concomitants build up in us a terrible need for security that we might survive. In time this need can become so great that we will seek security almost at any cost. Even little things we experience can register as threats to our survival and set off these tapes. Thus it sometimes happens that we step on someone's toe, and we get a reaction as if we had tried to cut off a head. The painful little incident was perceived as a threat to survival, and all the survival tapes started playing.

Well, we did survive. And we moved toward the wonderful, exciting twos. It is a time of adventure and discovery.

There comes the day when little Johnny discovers he has fingers. And Mother is delighted. And Daddy, too. I can remember my nephew saying how happy he was when his little one discovered she had a thumb and could put it in her mouth, relieving him of the oft repeated task of getting the pacifier there. Then little Johnny discovers he has toes and delights to play with them. And again mother is delighted. Then little Johnny discovers he has genitals and begins to delight in the sensations that he can produce there. And mother is horrified. Slap! Slap! "Don't touch that, you dirty little boy!" The little one in a very natural way is just seeking sensual and in a very primitive way sexual or, perhaps more rightly, genital pleasure. But it is encoded as something dirty and forbidden.

On top of this was, and still is for many I fear, the horror of toilet training. What should be the healthy and pleasurable experience of elimination is made into a shameful and painful discipline, coupled sometimes with many unreasonable scoldings and spankings.

And there were many other deprivations: things we were not to touch, not to taste, not to look at, not to experience in one way or another. And our natural reaching out for these things evoked a displeasure that was seen to threaten our security, our acceptance by those on whom we depended to provide our basic needs. All of this was registered in our memory and encoded on our memory tapes along with the emotions that were elicited. Thus there developed in us a great need for pleasure, pleasures of all kinds but most intimately and strongly the need for sensual and genital pleasure.

Our evolution went on. We became aware of the great wide world with all its threats as well as its possibilities. At the same time we became more and more aware that we belonged to a very particular group: the family. And we sought to find in this family, and especially in the strength of our fathers, the security force that would enable us to enter this world, face its danger, and enjoy its rich potentialities. But what happened in fact?

All too often today, the father is totally absent. Or, if physically present, he is emotionally and relationally absent, busy about other things, like building up his own false self by doing and acquiring. And unfortunately this can, all too often these days, also happen with the mother. It can also happen that, where the father is present, rather than his being there as an empowering presence, he is presented as a threatening force: "Wait till your father gets home. He will take care of you." And there we stand, little ones before a towering adult, who threatens to inflict pain or, at least, whose alienation threatens our secure living. There is a power vacuum in our lives and a desperate need for it to be filled. And again, all of this is registered in the memory along with all the emotional links. There is in us a terrible need for power.

And so here we stand, at the gateway to adulthood, expected to stand on our own two feet. We are supposed to think things through and make responsible decisions. But within us there churns a chaotic collection of emotion-laden needs: for basic survival and security, for pleasure, for acceptance and belonging and power. And who is here to help us sort all this out? Usually, no one. We cannot approach parents. They may well seem to be or are unapproachable. In any case they are too involved in it all. We talk with peers who are as mixed up as we are; they lead us into even more confusion.

I believe here is where the Church community most profoundly fails our young people and in the end ourselves, for we jeopardize and even loose our future. In the good old days, there was the extended family, and often there was in easy reach the sympathetic ear of a wise and kindly grandparent or aunt or uncle to whom we could turn. In school, even today there may be a teacher ready to listen and help, but for the most part teachers are too busy or fearful of possible consequences to open to such a personal relation with a student. The Church community needs to open free spaces for our young teenagers to hang out (far better than the malls and worse places to which they com-

71

monly gravitate) with wise and compassionate seniors from among us willing to hang around with open ears and hearts. Then maybe our young ones can find some of the help they need to sort through all these chaotic emotional needs.

Who else will point the emerging "I" toward community and even more toward Christ, the whole Christ, the community finding its fulfillment in Christ? This is the place where we find the fulfillment of all our aspirations, where we find true belonging and empowerment, security and eternal survival, the survival that goes beyond even the ultimate threat of death. In the absence of direction toward a healthy and healing community, confused young ones seek belonging and empowerment and even survival in gangs, look for pleasure in impulsive, irresponsible sex, in drugs and alcohol. And when all these fail, as they will, more and more young people seek oblivion in overdoses and suicide, often after expressing their anger in wreaking what vengeance they can on others.

We all see this played out in graphic detail in the lives of others. We need, perhaps, a bit of reflection to see how these deep emotional needs encoded on our memory tapes are playing themselves out in our own lives. We often do not realize what leads us to act the way we do. Or at times we are ashamed at the way we spontaneously act, yet we feel powerless to act otherwise — even those of us who have received the gift of faith and have entered into the community of Christ and see our destiny in Christ. Is there anything we can do about this? Or are we to remain helpless victims of our past?

The different schools of psychology have their different ways of expressing these realities and their different ways of attending to them, sometimes with useful insights. Among the schools is that of Jung, who hearkens back to Sigmund Freud and develops some of his insights. Among other things Freud found that if he could bring a person into a sense of security and then with suggestive words get the person to let the memory tapes run, the tapes could begin to play themselves out and the stored emotional drives could be released, dissipated, and even wiped out.

In a contemplative prayer like Centering Prayer, in faith and love we place ourselves securely in the most loving of hands. As we rest deeply in God in the center, memories are left free to surface. If we become aware of them we simply, gently return to the Lord at the center and let them run on, for we know if we begin to work with them we will only reencode them. As they float away they carry with them some of the emotional gunk that surrounded them. Little by little the emotional drives for security and survival, for pleasure, for belonging and power are dissipated and the memories are healed. We come to a new freedom. Every little threat no longer calls up a desperate need for security and survival. The emotional need for sensual and genital pleasure, for a sense of power abates. The insights of faith can begin to prevail. Through the experience of God we come to know the deeper and more perduring pleasures or joy of the spirit, we know we belong, we can do all things in the God who strengthens us, we have eternal life.

We have all had a rough journey. But with the healing of memories and the confident hope we have of possessing all in Christ, of attaining to Omega consciousness, to the Omega Point, we can move ahead with a certain enthusiasm and excitement. The more this healing is complemented by the actual experience of God in the Prayer, the more powerful is our hope.

We know: The best is yet to come.

S I X

A Living Heritage

The Lord gives the word
to the bearers of good tidings.

—Psalm 67

Every great wisdom tradition has flowed forth from the
experience of a particular person or persons. Some of
these sages are completely wrapped in myth: Krishna,
Ram. Others have been able to preserve their historical identity even as life-giving myth enfolded them:
Buddha, Abraham, Moses. The great Rabbi, Jesus the
Christ, Incarnate Wisdom in the flesh, brought the
richness of his Jewish heritage to a new fullness in
the way of transcending and transforming love. When
this heritage was in danger of being engulfed by a pa-
tronizing world, after the conversion of Constantine
the Great in the fourth century, many of it greatest
teachers took refuge in the deserts. And true seekers

75

flocked to these fathers and mothers of the desert and brought their wisdom back, weaving it into the living fabric of the Church, especially through the monastic orders.

This rich heritage has lived on and finds its expression in one of the great spiritual masters of our century, Father M. Louis of Gethsemani, Thomas Merton. When he received a call from the Lord and responded to it to enter into the Cistercian way, with his exceptional genius, Father Louis opened himself to the master of the Cistercian school, Bernard of Clairvaux. He drew from Bernard this master's insightful teaching on the false and true self. In his first published volume, *The Spirit of Simplicity,* Father Louis brought together what is Bernard's final and fullest expression of his teaching on this.

Merton lived in the context of a very defensive and rationalistic post-Tridentine Church. Spiritual teaching had become encased in programs that can all too easily become projects of the false self. So-called spiritual directors guided disciples step by step up the mountain or through the rooms of the interior castle. Progress was clearly mapped. It became a skilled undertaking. Nonetheless the true masters, the great spiritual fathers and mothers, were still able to share their wisdom in transcendent poetry and the intuitions of homey details.

The poet in Father Louis responded to and was enlivened by these great poetic endeavors. He tried also to submit to the straits of the projects. This resulted in a period of writer's block, if not a full-scale nervous breakdown. He passed beyond this, and, inspirited by the wisdom of Bernard, he was able to produce his own finest theological expression of the richness of this tradition in his book *The New Man*. He himself had become a new man.

Years before, as a lively and very gifted young man, Merton bought into the false self quite fully. He rose from a crash at Cambridge to become the big man around campus at Columbia University, New York. But he had too much insight and God-given grace not to see the hollowness of this. He searched for something more, for an authenticity, a trueness that would correspond to and fulfill his deepest instincts.

At this early stage in his life he saw the possibility of living an authentic life in two different ways which for him were standing in an excluding opposition. Inspired by Catherine de Hueck, he went to the slums of New York City and sought to raise social consciousness by actually living with the disenfranchised and serving them. During the same period, a visit to Gethsemani opened for him the beauty of the contemplative way. It would only be many years later, after he had been freed from the imperious demands of a false self, that he would see through this false dichotomy. He not only used his gifts as a writer to contribute much to the raising of social consciousness, but he came to know with conviction that the contemplation of the individual is a powerful leaven, raising the consciousness of the whole human family. Only with time would he be able to say that "to live well myself is my first and essential contribution to the well-being of all mankind and to the fulfillment of man's [and woman's] collective destiny." He also came to see that the contemplative community not only gave witness to this but stood as a clear witness to many of the social values of a truly Christian life. If Thomas Merton had decided to pursue a life of witness and service to the poor and disenfranchised by joining Catherine de Hueck at Friendship House in the slums of Harlem, we can well wonder whether he would have ever come to the prominence that enabled him to use his pen so effectively to raise the social consciousness of multitudes in the United States and in other countries as well.

After an intense personal struggle Merton opted for a vocation to the Cistercian way. This was not done with a wholly pure heart. Indeed it could have been in part motivated by the fact that Japan had just attacked the United States and working for the poor in Harlem would not have saved him from being drafted into the army. But he never admitted to this motive for heading to the monastery the day after war was declared. What he did admit to was a certain compromise in regards to his aspirations to be recognized as a writer and in particular as a poet. While he did dispose of some of his writings, others he stored with his friend Mark van Doren (the day would come when he would reclaim them), and he brought with him to the monastery a collection of poems. This led to a drama that makes us smile with a groan.

After he was settled in the novitiate for a time, Tom one day took his collection of poems to his father master, Robert McGann, who later became abbot of Holy Trinity Abbey in Utah. When Tom entered the room, Father Walter, the submaster and later abbot of Genesee Abbey, was also there. With great diffidence Tom laid his precious collection on the father master's desk: I thought you might like to see some of my poetry. A breezy blessing dismissed the novice.

As the door closed behind him, the novice master exclaimed: "Poetry, indeed!" And forthwith deposited the collection in the wastebasket.

Fortunately, Tom had an abbot who, like his mother, had come from a literary family in Ohio. This wise and holy man knew that the Cistercian way could indeed embrace a fruitful literary output. Were not many of the first Cistercian fathers magnificent writers. This good abbot took steps toward helping Tom integrate his literary gifts into his Cistercian life. This led to the production of one of the most influential pieces of Christian literature in this century: *The Seven Storey Mountain.*

With whatever degree of purity of heart he did have and certainly with a great deal of sincerity this young teacher pursued the Cistercian way. But the ever-cunning false self was not to be defeated so easily. Soon enough all the young aspirant's energies were flowing into the creation of a new false self, that of the perfect monk. It was this that drove Louis into the ways of a project-oriented spirituality and perfected monastic image. Early pictures of the ascetic young monk remind one of the survivors of Auschwitz. It was only after seventeen years the breakthrough came, for God will not let good zeal, no matter how misguided, go unrewarded: Seek and you shall find.

Merton recounts this breakthrough most completely and concisely in a letter. If you really want to get to know Merton, the place to go is to his letters. He was a copious letter-writer. And a very good one. Graham Greene, after exchanging a number of letters with Father Louis in regard to the British edition of the *Seven Storey Mountain,* urged the young monk to give up other kinds of writings and devote himself exclusively to letter writing. His letters flowed directly from his heart, through his battered little typewriter, right to the recipient. Unlike the journals, they were not written with an eye toward publication. And the more deeply Louis sensed a spiritual affinity with his recipient and the further away the recipient was the more totally did Merton reveal himself.

Thus it is in a letter to Boris Pasternak, which would take months to arrive through the underground to the recipient on the other side of the globe, that Louis shares most openly this significant event:

It is a simple enough story, but obviously I do not tell it to people — you are the fourth who knows it and there seems to be no point in a false discretion that might restrain me from telling you since it is clear that we have so very much in common. One night [February 28, 1958] I dreamt that I was sitting with a very young Jewish girl of fourteen or fifteen, and that she suddenly manifested a very deep affection for me and embraced me so that I was moved to the depths of my soul. I learned that her name was "Proverb," which I thought very simple and beautiful. And also I thought, "She is of the race of St. Anne." I spoke to her of her name, and she did not seem to be proud of it, because it seemed rather the other young girls mocked her for it. But I told her that it was a very beautiful name, and there the dream ended. A few days later when I happened to be in a nearby city [March 18, in Louisville], which is very rare for us, I was walking alone in the crowded street and suddenly saw that everybody was Proverb and that in all of them shone her extraordinary beauty and purity and shyness, even though they did not know who they were and were perhaps ashamed of their names — because they were mocked on account of them. And they did not know their real identity as the Child so dear to God who, from before the beginning, was playing in His sight all days, playing in the world.

Merton adds with humor: "Thus you are initiated into the scandalous secret of a monk who is in love with a girl and a Jew at that! One cannot expect much from monks these days. The heroic asceticism of the past is no more."

Humor often hides truth. Merton no longer sought to be a heroic ascetic, a model monk, but rather a man of love, of compassion, of presence, even if the righteous were scandalized. Merton brings this out in his more sober and less intimate account of the experience in his published journal, *Conjectures of a Guilty Bystander:*

In Louisville, at the corner of Fourth and Walnut in the center of the shopping district, I was suddenly overwhelmed with the realization that I loved all those people, that they were mine and I theirs, that we could not be alien to one another even though we were total strangers. It was like awaking from a dream of separate-ness, of spurious self-isolation in a special world, the world of renunciation and supposed holiness.

83

And he goes on to share something of what the experience meant for him:

This sense of liberation from an illusory difference was such a relief and such a joy to me that I almost laughed out loud. And I suppose my happiness could have taken form in the words: "Thank God, thank God that I am like other men, that I am only a man among others." To think that for sixteen or seventeen years I have been taking seriously this pure illusion. . . .

It is a glorious destiny to be a member of the human race. . . . Now I realize what we all are. And if only everybody could realize this. But it cannot be explained. There is no way of telling people that they are all walking around shining like the sun. . . .

If only they could all see themselves as they really *are*. If only we could see each other that way all the time. There would be no more war, no more hatred, no more cruelty, no more greed. . . . I suppose the big problem would be that we would fall down and worship each other. But this cannot be *seen*, only believed and "under-stood" by a peculiar gift. . . .

At the center of our being is a point of nothingness which is untouched by sin and by illusions, a point of pure truth, a point or spark which belongs entirely to God, which is never at our disposal, from which God disposes our lives, which is inaccessible to the fantasies of our own mind or the brutalities of our own will. This little point of nothingness and of *absolute poverty* is the pure glory of God in us. It is so to speak His name written in us, as our poverty, as our indigence, as our dependence, as our sonship. It is like a pure diamond, blazing with the invisible light of heaven. It is in everybody, and if we could see it we would see these billions of points of light coming together in the face and blaze of a sun that would make all the darkness and cruelty of life vanish completely. . . . I have no program for this seeing. It is only given. But the gate of heaven is everywhere.

Having gone through this profoundly significant experience, Father Louis could now write in *New Seeds of Contemplation:*

For me to become a saint means to be myself. Therefore the problem of sanctity and salvation is in fact the problem of finding out who I am and of discovering my true self. Trees and animals have no problem. God makes them what they are without consulting them, and they are perfectly satisfied. With us it is different. God leaves us free to become whatever we like. We can be ourselves or not, as we please. We are at liberty to be real or to be unreal. We may be true or false, the choice is ours. We may wear now one mask and now another, and never, if we so desire, appear with our own true face. But we cannot make choices with impunity. Causes have effects, and if we lie to ourselves and to others, then we cannot expect to find truth and reality whenever we happen to want them. If we have chosen the way of falsity we must not be surprised that truth eludes us when we finally come to need it. We are called to share with God in creating our true identity.

Celebrating the true self, Merton could now clearly put his finger on the false self:

This false, exterior, superficial, social self is made up of prejudices, whimsy, posturing, pharisaic self-concern and pseudo dedication. The false self is a human construct built by selfishness and flights from reality. Because it is not the whole truth of us, it is not of God. And because it is not of God, our false self is substantially empty and incapable of experiencing the love and freedom of God.

With this experience Father Louis knew a new freedom and joy; he could move ahead into the fullness of his true self. There was a new assurance in his writing. The richness of the Cistercian heritage now belonged to him in a new way, and he could give it his own contemporary expression in *The New Man*. Here he rarely uses the terminology of the true and false self but rather, "following the thought of St. Bernard," he resorts to the more biblical terminology of the image and likeness. We lost the likeness, went off into the land of unlikeness, and have to make our way back to our native true likeness.

As he would write in a later introduction:

There is in us an instinct... for renewal, for a liberation of creative power... which tells us that this change is a recovery of that which is deepest, most original, more personal in ourselves. To be born again is not to become somebody different, but to become ourselves.

In *The New Man* he develops his insight most fully:

It is a spiritual disaster for a man [or woman] to rest content with his exterior identity, with his passport picture of himself. Is his life merely in his fingerprints? Does he really exist because his name has been inscribed in *Who's Who?* Is his picture in the Sunday paper any safe indication that he is not a zombie? If that is who he thinks he is, then he is already done for, because he is no longer alive, even though he may seem to exist. Actually he is only pushing the responsibility for his existence on to society. Instead of facing the question of who he is, he assumes he is a person because there appear to be other persons who recognize him when he walks down the street.

Since we are made in the image and likeness of God, there is no other way for us to find out who we are than by finding in ourselves the divine image. Now this image, which is present in every one of us by nature, can indeed be known by rational inference. But that is not enough to give us a real experience of our own identity. It is hardly better than inferring that we exist because other people act as if we existed.

Just as some men have to struggle to recover a natural, spontaneous realization of their own capacity for life and movement and physical enjoyment, so all men have to struggle to regain the spontaneous and vital awareness of their spirituality, of the fact that they have a soul that is capable of coming to life and experiencing profound and hidden values which the flesh and its senses can never discover alone. And this spirituality in man is identified with the divine image in our soul.

Now if we are to recognize this image in ourselves, it is not sufficient for us to enter into ourselves. It is not enough for us to realize that the spirituality of our nature makes us potentially God-like. The potentiality must be actualized. How? By knowledge and love: or, more precisely, by a knowledge of God that is inseparable from an experience of love....

Self-realization in this true religious sense is then less an awareness of ourselves than it is an awareness of the God to whom we are drawn in the depths of our own being. We become real, and experience our actuality, not when we pause to reflect upon our own self as an isolated individual entity, but rather when, transcending ourselves and passing beyond reflection, we center our whole soul upon the God who is our life. That is to say we fully "realize" ourselves when we cease to be conscious of ourselves in separateness and know nothing but the one God who is above all knowledge. We fully realize ourselves when all our awareness is of another, of Him who is utterly "Other" than all beings because He is infinitely above them. The image of God is brought to life in us when it breaks free from the shroud and the tomb in which our self-consciousness had kept it prisoner, and loses itself in a total consciousness of Him who is Holy. This is one of the main ways in which "he that would save his life will lose it. . . ."

The recovery of the divine image in our souls, insofar as it is experienced by us at all, is an experience of a totally new manner of being. We become "new men" in Christ, and we are able to verify the fact by the change in the object of our knowledge and in our manner of knowing. Indeed, when God is known in this sense,

He is not known as an "object" since He is not contained in a concept. On the contrary, the mystical knowledge of God, actualized in the mirror of His image within us mysteriously coincides with His knowledge of us: "I shall know," says St. Paul, "even as I have been known." We apprehend Him by the love which identifies itself, within us, with His love for us. What will be fully realized in the beatific vision is realized inchoatively in contemplation even in this present life.

The recognition of our true self, in the divine image, is then a recognition of the fact that we are known and loved by God. As such it is utterly different from any self-awareness, no matter how deeply spiritual it may seem. It is utterly different from any other kind of spiritual awakening, except perhaps the awakening of life that takes place within a man when he suddenly discovers that he is indeed loved by another human being. Yet this human awakening is only a faint analogue of the divine awakening that takes place when the "image" in our spirit comes to itself and realizes that it has been "seen" and "called" by God, and that its destiny is to be carried toward Him.

Without this inner awakening, which springs from the realization of God's merciful love for us, the image remains a mere potential likeness, buried and obscured, unappreciated because unseen. The image springs to life when, at the touch of God's ineffable mercy, it begins to take on its lost likeness to Him who is Love. The presence of God in us is the presence of His likeness in our own spirit — a likeness which is more than a representation, it is the Word of God Himself, united to our soul by the action of His Spirit. The sense of being "carried" and "drawn" by love into the infinite space of a sublime and unthinkable freedom is the expression of our spiritual union with the Father, in the Son, and by the Holy Ghost, which constitutes us in our true identity as sons [and daughters] of God.

All of this is, as Merton's title indicates, an elaboration of the Pauline text:

You are to put off your old self with its way of life which is corrupted through illusion and desire and take on a fresh new way of knowing in the Spirit so that you may put on the New Man created in God's image, whose rightness and holiness are born of Truth.

To let Father Louis put it very succinctly: "We are only really ourselves when we completely consent to 'receive' the glory of God into ourselves."

The sudden and tragic death of Father Louis in Bangkok in 1968 brought an end to the evolution of this wisdom tradition within this great spirit. But the evolution itself among the People of God goes on. The development of doctrine and teaching has moved ahead in another great Cistercian master, Father Thomas Keating, abbot-emeritus of Spencer. Father Thomas has not hesitated to draw from the wisdom and insights of the behavioral sciences, which have made such strides in our times, to enrich his presentation of the spiritual journey. Some of his wisdom is reflected, authentically and fruitfully I hope, in this small volume.

Father Louis emphasized the painful side, in a way I have not, of letting go of the false self:

The difficult ascent from falsity toward truth is accomplished not through pleasant advances in wisdom and insight, but through the painful unlayering of levels of falsehood, untruths deeply embedded in our consciousness, lies which cling more tightly than a second skin.

Only when we have descended in dread to the center of our nothingness, by His grace and His guidance can we be led by Him, in His own time, to find Him in losing ourselves.

For the way to God lies through deep darkness in which all knowledge and all created wisdom and all pleasure and prudence and all human hope and human joy are defeated and annulled by the overwhelming purity of the light of the presence of God.

I believe when we choose the path of contemplative prayer much of the pain is relieved. The transformation becomes more fully and directly God's work. And we progress with a quiet assurance both as to the reality of that toward which we move, the true self, and as to the fact that, with God's help and doing, it will be fully achieved.

Nonetheless as one moves along we are confronted with the falseness of some of the things we do, of the phoniness of displaying certain possessions, of the repeatedly gnawing concern about what others are going to think, catching ourselves in deceptive and secretive behavior. We find ourselves knowing our captivity, experiencing the shame, wanting the liberty, and still fearing the cost: What will people think? As I suggested before, it is wonderful to be able to have the humor to laugh at ourselves each time we catch ourselves seeking to construct this false self. Then we can move ahead peacefully and humbly.

It does take a certain simplicity to trustfully and confidently follow the path of contemplation, knowing that in God's good time, with our cooperation, God will complete the work and bring us to that uniquely beautiful Truth that God has ever enjoyed in the eternal NOW. Merton saw this clearly; he tells us that the realization of the true self "means that we become transformed from within by God's inner Presence in order to become like God, living in God, seeing as God sees, loving as God loves all creation — with compassion. God does it in us, not we."

Yes, it is God's work. And it is ours. And it is an ever ongoing pursuit. As Merton so well says: "Perfection is rather a pursuit, ever moving forward, deeper into the mystery of God . . . and each fulfillment contains in itself the impulse to further exploration."

SEVEN

By Every Word

We have already seen how Jesus, at the very beginning of his saving mission, was tempted to create a false self, by doing, by having, by establishing himself in the estimation of others. And we have seen that he clearly and unhesitatingly rejected this. Jesus knew his true self. His hours of silent communion with the Father, with Abba, flowed from this and at the same time left no doubt in his mind about this. "The Father and I are one." "The one who sees me, sees the Father."

As he faced temptation and responded to the tempter, Jesus, the master, our teacher, indicated yet another way, one at the rational level, which enables us to uncover the deceits of the false self. Jesus responded to the alluring deceptions of the evil one with the all-powerful Word of God. "Scripture says: 'Human beings live not on bread alone, but on every word that comes from the mouth of God.'" Indeed, his chosen disciple would later remind the faithful: "Every word was written for our instruction."

Here we have another antidote to the false self: a daily feeding, a steady immersion into the Word of God. When we are daily fed by the Word of God, when it nourishes us and nurtures us, it forms our mind and heart in Truth. It uncovers and peels away, one by one, the deceptions of the false self. It grounds us in the Truth and enables us to discern, in the light of that Truth, our true selves in the truth of our relationship with God. At the same time it becomes the vehicle by which we are able to bring back into everyday life at the rational level the experience of Truth that we have in contemplative prayer.

The devil — and the false self — is quick to turn everything to his devious service, even the Word of God. After Jesus' decisive rejection of the first temptation with the Word, the tempter takes up the Word to deliver his second temptation: "Throw yourself down, for Scripture says: 'He has given his angels....'" A daily exposure to the Truth of the Word should lead us ever more clearly into that truth which Jesus expressed in his response to the third temptation: "The Lord your God is the one to whom you must do homage. God alone you must serve" — and not some false self.

Unfortunately we can turn our daily encounter with the Word into something we "do" to make us a person. We are back in the false self, seeking to find an identity in what we do. And, as we go about our daily reading, we can also collect texts and wonderful insights. Soon we have an impressive collection. We can bring forth the right word at the right time. We have it! "I am the one who has it." Again, we are constructing the false self by having.

If we seek to live by the Words that come forth from the mouth of God, they can uncover the deceits of the false self, they can bring us into a knowledge of the true self and nourish that self. But it is important how we approach the Word in order to allow it to do this, to truly nourish us and form us.

The traditional way to do this, the way that comes to us through the living tradition of the Christian community, is called, by that same tradition, *lectio divina.*

Lectio is very different from what we understand today as reading: allowing markings on a page, symbols, to convey to our mind, through the eye, certain concepts or ideas. Lectio is an openness to a more integral hearing that will bring us beyond conceptual knowledge to the experience of Reality.

Our Lord has told us: Unless you become as a little child, you will not enter in. Certainly this Man, who walked steadfastly to the cross and told his disciples that we must take up our cross daily and follow, this Man who withstood the powers of his times and sent his disciples forth to teach all nations, was not calling us to childishness.

The human intellect in its reception of truth has two modes of functioning. There is the discursive or empirical function that gathers data and engages in deductive thinking. It tends to try to fit everything into its pattern of thinking, to master its subject. It is prone to engender pride and, among other things, it can lead to ecological disaster. When we see everything in creation as something we are to master, and therefore to use as we want in our service without respect for its own inner nature and the overall plan of the Creator, then we have a formula for disaster. Yet when the human mind functions in this way it is called "being rational," as if to imply any other mode was irrational.

Another mode of functioning for the human intellect is the contemplative or intuitive or sapiential function. Here the intellect gathers its data by intuition and insight and proceeds by way of relational thinking. Rather than fitting the data into its established parameters, it opens itself to allow the data to expand them. Such a way of functioning calls for humility and engenders humility. It is here that the mythological finds its home; myth which brings to us those truths which are too big to be fitted into our rational concepts, the concepts which we have created.

The child, whose physical brain and rational functions are still in their initial stages of development, is open to receiving stories with their full mythological content without the judgmental hindrance of the discursive intellect. Children enter fully into the experience even when they have little understanding of its meaning. Their minds, their imaginations, their emotions are being formed, even as the experience is registered in the storehouse of the memory.

When Jesus calls us to be childlike, he is calling upon us to use our intuitive or sapiential function, to be open to the stories, the myths, that convey to us the truth of the Revelation which has a fullness beyond that which our rationally formed concepts can grasp. By the images and stories of the divinely inspired Scriptures God transmits to us some knowledge of Godself and of God's way of seeing the creation.

101

The open mind is expanded. It humbly points beyond itself, giving direction to the heart. As Thomas Aquinas said: Where the mind leaves off, the heart goes beyond. We open ourselves to what the fathers call "love-knowledge," that experiential knowledge that comes to us through the intuitions of love. Such an openness alone enables us to receive with ever increasing fullness the Truth that the Word of God has been divinely inspired to bring to us.

Wise parents, wishing to form their children in the faith, will see that from the very beginning their storybooks include Bible stories; that their video library includes the many wonderful cartoon presentations of the Bible stories and the life of Christ and also the stories of his saints. The child will not at first discern any difference between these and the other stories which are a product of the human mind and imagination, between the story of the Lion King and that of Samson or Judith or Christ himself. But as the discursive function develops, enlightened by faith, the young person can be guided into a discernment whereby the images and intuitions that have come from the stories of the Revelation will become the operative guides in their lives.

If we Christians are to retain a certain childlike quality in our approach to God in general, it is especially important that this be so in our openness to the Revelation as it comes to us in the Sacred Scriptures. It is a quality of true lectio.

In the beginning of the sixth century Benedict of Nursia wrote his *Rule for Monasteries*. Today it is the rule by which most of the monastics of the West seek to live. Significantly in this rule there is no mention of meditation or contemplation. Benedict does make ample provision for lectio: two hours early in the day most of the year, three hours in Lent, plus another short period in the evening. In the twelfth century, by the time that the more rationalistic approach of scholasticism had begun to prevail in the Church, Guigo II the Carthusian clearly distinguished what he calls the four "steps": lectio, meditation, prayer, and contemplation. Climbing these steps, he sees the human mind at labor to grasp and take possession of what it receives in lectio and to think it through. Lectio and meditation have become in practice very much sacred study.

Sacred study is an important element in our lives. We are to love the Lord our God with our whole mind. We need to apply ourselves, to press our edges, in our effort to understand the Revelation through the study of the Scriptures. Great advances have been made in the field of scriptural studies. And also, unfortunately, some rather ridiculous and arrogant humanistic and anthropocentric dissections of the Sacred Text have taken place which also claim to be scriptural studies. We need not waste time giving any attention to these latter. But the rich fruit of genuine Scripture scholarship can help us to receive more fully the Revelation the Lord wishes to impart to us through his inspired Text.

Let me just interject one example of an instance which was very meaningful to me. At the present time the majority of the scholars are agreed that the meal which the Lord Jesus celebrated with his chosen Twelve on the night before he died was indeed a Seder meal, a meal in celebration of the Passover. It followed the age-old sacred ritual which would have been familiar to Jesus and his friends since their early youth when as the youngest among those gathered they would have been called upon to ask the ritual questions. However, on that eventful evening Jesus introduced into this most sacred meal the initiation of a new covenant. When he, as the master of the table, took bread and blessed it and gave it to his disciples, he said, "This is my Body," changing the bread into his very self.

There are in the course of this ritual meal four cups of benediction. At each, each one at the table takes up his own cup while the master of the table says the blessing and then each drinks from his own cup. At this particular meal, Jesus took up the cup for the fourth benediction and said the blessing. Then he went on to say: "This is the cup of my blood, the blood of the new and everlasting covenant. Take this all of you and drink from it." And then, instead of each drinking from his own cup, Jesus' cup was passed around and each drank from the one cup, his cup. Study brings home to us this profoundly significant change in the ritual. We all drink of one cup, of Jesus' cup, because we now know that we are now one, one in him.

Sacred study will till and fertilize our minds, by its disciplines removing the stones and briars, making our minds fertile ground to receive the seed of the Word. But it is a perduring openness that allows the seed to enter in and then do its thing so that new life can spring forth. The mind does not want to crush the seed like earth packed hard by many feet or stunt its growth by confining it within the stones and brambles of our own thoughts and concepts.

We do need to do what study we can to prepare

the soil. And we also need to do some "spiritual" or motivational reading to give direction to our lives and encourage the openness and responsiveness we need for lectio. But of themselves study and active intellectual reading will do little to bring about a transformation of our consciousness, little to expose the false self and give birth to the true self. If our lectio is reduced to such exercises, it will not be the force for transformation it is meant to be. True lectio does need to be clearly distinguished from these other kinds of sacred reading or intellectual endeavor.

In true lectio we allow the Word of God to come in, to do its work within and to bring us to God consciousness. This is why Benedict did not need to speak specifically of meditation or contemplation. He allowed ample periods when the readers opened themselves to the Word and allowed it to bring the mind down into the heart (meditation) and open out into an experiential love-knowledge of the Divine Word (contemplation). It was one inclusive encounter with the Word.

It is true that for such lectio, lectio in the fullest meaning of the word, we do need a certain amount of gracious space in the time we can give to it. When this is not possible and our lectio time must be quite

106

limited, even severely so, we need to weave the process into our lives. In the brief time we are able to be with the Sacred Text, we want to be wide open, receiving the seed of the Word. Then as we go about our day, we want to let the Word go with us, continuing its work within us — meditation. And we provide for other time, when we can let everything else go and let the Word bring us freely and fully into the experience of God. In this way, even the most active of lives can preserve and enjoy a contemplative dimension.

When we come to lectio, then, it is very important we come with a contemplative attitude, even if the time we can allow ourselves here and now for lectio is very brief. We need to come with faith: This is the Word of God. God is here in his Word. I come not to collect words. And certainly not to master the Word. But to receive it and to be mastered, formed and transformed by this Word.

We need to be profoundly aware that this is God's work, the work of the Spirit of God. It was Holy Spirit who inspired those who put these words on paper for the Church. It is Holy Spirit who lives within us to teach us all things and to bring to mind all that Jesus has taught us. We humbly and ardently seek the help of the Spirit and depend on Holy Spirit all through our time of lectio and beyond, as we carry this Word through our ongoing life.

We need to leave aside that active mind that would seek to take control of every word, every thought that enters, evaluate it and fit it into our previously constructed framework. Concepts of God we may be able to fit into a *Summa theologiae* but, as Aquinas learned, not God's very Self. In lectio we are not seeking to collect or create concepts about God. We want God in God's very Self. We do not want to embrace ideas; we want to be embraced and brought to new levels of knowledge, levels beyond the rational, that love-knowledge that brings us into Divine Knowledge, the experience of the Truth who is God.

We want to be wholly in act in our loving receptivity. Lectio is not passive. In our act of love, we are totally there, leaving behind all self-initiated activity of the mind, memory, and imagination. Like a good dancer, we totally move with our Partner, letting God lead us into movements and rhythms, levels of experience and excitement beyond anything the rational mind can conceive, beyond all the flights of our imagination: "Eye has not seen, ear has not heard, nor has it entered into the human mind what God has prepared for those who love God. But Holy Spirit makes it known to us."

Lectio in its fullness is contemplation. And as such it brings about in us a transformation of consciousness. The false self with all its constructs is left behind. What we have now, if I can use the word "have" here, is not anything we can do or possess. It is not anything we can of ourselves in any way express or show to win the acceptance or admiration of others. It simply is. And leaves us profoundly humble, profoundly fulfilled, profoundly happy.

I have always seen in Mary, the Mother of our Lord, the exemplar and model of truest Christian living. At the very beginning, when she is entering into her role as Mother of God, I believe Mary exemplifies true lectio.

We do not know what Mary was engaged in at the moment of the Annunciation. We have no idea just how the angel "appeared" to her. But there was an openness here to an astounding Word.

Just think of Mary here. A young maiden, probably she would have appeared to us no more than a girl. Had she ever left her village, a village at the end of the world, so to speak? "Can anything good come out of Nazareth?" was a common adage. And what was her life like in the village? A life full of everyday, humdrum details. The only big event of the week was going to the synagogue. And even here the role of the women was subdued, to say the least, as they clustered behind their grills. They heard the Word of God, they sang the Word of God, they celebrated the Word of God. They carried the Word of God home in their minds and hearts. If they were to learn to read and write — a rare enough thing, especially for a woman — it was from the Word of God.

Mary's whole life was embraced by the Word of God, by the Jewish ethos. And what was central in all this? There is one God, and that God is our God.

Well, this messenger arrives from on high. Angelic messengers were not such a rarity in her tradition, but there was absolutely nothing in Mary's past that could have prepared her intellectually for the message that was brought to her: God, your God, the God of Abraham, Moses, and David, your father, this God has a Son. God has a Son! If this was not enough to blow all the fuses of a well-formed Jewish mind, the messenger goes on to tell this young woman: And God wants you to be the mother of this Son. Even if Mary had not gone through a painful discernment process and had been led to see her special call to be a virgin daughter of God and then more wondrously found a man who could understand and enter into a participation in such a vocation — even if all this were not so, what could a young Jewish maiden do with this Revelation?

We know what happened. Mary did not question the Revelation. She did question how she was to respond cooperatively to it. She remained open and let the power of this revealing Word expand her mind and heart so that in some way she could give a fully human "yes" to what was being asked of her. In essence there was being revealed to her the two central mysteries of our Christian faith: the Trinity and the Incarnation. How the parameters of her mind had to give way to allow space for these mysteries to enter into her consciousness. Indeed a transformation of consciousness was taking place, though in this case not from a false self to a true self but from a lived Promise to an astounding fulfillment: And the Word was made flesh and dwelt among us.

When we come to lectio we want to come with the openness of Mary, ready to let all the parameters of our consciousness go and to let the Word of God expand us to a wholly new consciousness, ultimately a God-consciousness. When we consistently so expose ourselves to the Truth, the false self cannot long remain in control. It will not so easily die. It will fight all the way and use every ruse it can to get the upper hand, even like the devil using the Word itself. It will try to make our lectio into something we "do" to make ourselves good and of some worth in the eyes of God and more enlightened humans. It will try to gather up the insights we get in the course of our lectio and make all that something we "have," again to give us some worth. And it can show them off to win the admiration and approval of others: "Boy, does she know Scripture!" But as we return again and again, in the spirit of true lectio, to the very Truth revealed, this false self with all its phoniness will wither and die. At the same time, as the light of the Truth shines upon us with ever increasing clarity, we will perceive in the Truth our true self and the trueness of every other human person and of the whole creation in our oneness in the creative and redemptive act of the Divine.

EIGHT

A Farewell Word: Love Is God's Being

We are fortunate to be living in a time when the evolution of human consciousness has reached the challenging level that it has, when science is making wondrous strides. Today science often makes more progress in a year, gains more insights, than it did in a decade at the beginning of this century, than it did in a century at the dawning of the second millennium.

As we saw earlier, great medieval theologians, like John of Damascus and Thomas Aquinas, saw the creation as God reaching out and going out as far as God could from Godself to create inert matter, pure potential — the very opposite of God who is pure spirit, pure act. Science now reveals to us that the basic building block of creation, the beginning of the evolution of human consciousness, is not inert matter but vibrant chaotic energy. Matter in fact is bound and condensed energy. And if this energy were to be released suddenly and allowed to act in its own uncontrolled way, it has the potential for untold destruction. This was amply demonstrated to us when the atomic bomb was diabolically exploded above the crowded cathedral in Nagasaki that Sunday morning. This immense chaotic energy which is, as it were, a sea upon which all the matter that we experience floats and out of which it all emerges is harnessed and organized by some mysterious force that brings out of its vibrant and violent power its ever evolving beings.

No wonder the ancients who touched in some way this reality stood in terror before the forces of nature, perceived a divinity in them, and sought to placate them. As our human consciousness evolved, the Divine, as it were, took steps toward us and revealed more and more the fullness of Reality. The lightning and thunder of Sinai was easier for the earlier recipients of the Revelation to accept as a Divine experience. It was only in the fullness of time that God was able to reveal to us — who by the grace of the evolution began to have ears that could hear — that this energy that is the source of all and is in all is in fact love, a tender, all-embracing love within which we live and move and have our being.

114

Love is what matters because God is love. Every love is an expression of God. And God has used every means to bring this home to us, beginning already in the very work of creation and then in the earliest moments of the Revelation where God walks arm in arm with Adam under the trees of Eden. If God's Song of Songs sung by his wise servant Solomon was literally cast it would undoubtedly be an X-rated movie so sensuously erotic is its expressions of love as God seeks to bring home to us how much God does love. With the fullness of Revelation in Christ Jesus came the greatest sign of love: Greater love than this no one has than that one lay down one's life for one's friend. The horror of Calvary, which engraves itself upon our minds, imaginations, and hearts, is meant to be the most vivid proclamation of love that creation will ever witness.

The noted and profoundly religious Jewish writer Chaim Potok, in his character Asher Lev, shocks his Jewish audience by choosing the crucifixion to express the greatest love the young artist knew, the suffering patient love of his mother for his father. In the drama of Asher Lev, Potok brings forth the fundamental challenge that we each live. Asher had to decide whether to live out the fullness of his love in what is ordinarily naturally most precious to a man, his son, devoting himself to the education (in the fullest sense of that word) of that son within the religious community or to unleash the powerful forces within him that lay in his artistic gifts. In the end the artist decides to go with his art, giving his son up to his own, totally devoted father and their religious community. And with that choice he experiences the forces within him driving him to create paintings that the critics found hard to comprehend and deeply disturbing precisely because they were seeking to express the chaotic primal energy within us.

The author of *The Cloud of Unknowing*, as he instructs his spiritual son, passes on from the Tradition a simple method for entering into communion with the primal forces of Divine Love within, which communion is contemplative prayer. He tells his son to choose a simple, single-syllable word that meaningfully expresses the Reality. And he suggests to him two alternatives: God and love. God, the tri-personal, is beyond the personal. This is one of the insights that today's feminist theology is setting powerfully before us. God is beyond male and female, Father and Mother. The challenge here is to move with this without losing the power that the personal expressions of our relationship with God have for us. This great

116

contemplative, the anonymous author of *The Cloud*, coming from his lived experience, knew that God is love, that the vibrant energy of the Divine that expresses itself in the creation is with all its chaotic power an all-embracing, most tender and caring love. It is the vulnerable love that Jesus sought to express in the touching stories of the Good Shepherd and the Prodigal Father.

Sadly, it is indeed difficult for us who have grown up with these stories and in the whole Christian atmosphere to realize how shocking such images of God were to Jesus' Jewish audience. "No man ever spoke as this man." To portray God as an anguished father who, after he had given his son his freedom, would suffer the consequences of the misuse of that freedom is a profoundly disturbing image of the terrible and terrifying God of Sinai, the majestic God of Solomon's magnificent temple. To see, as it were, God's happiness dependent upon our conversion is mystery indeed. To see God going out not only to the obviously messed-up sinner who has turned back repentant but even to the self-righteous but hurting jealous son — these profoundly human images invite us to enter more and more into the mystery of an awesome chaotic energy that is harnessed as love.

The first man and woman were created in the image and likeness of God. There resided in them not only the Divine Creative Energy but that Energy in them was wholly love. When that love turned back upon itself in selfishness, it lost its likeness to God. The image ever remained. We are ever an expression of the Divine Creative Energies. But the likeness was lost. We were no longer an energy that is love and that brings energy through chaos into unity and peace. Thus chaos takes hold of our lives and our world. At baptism the Divine Spirit who is Love, the Love of the First Person of the Trinity for the Second and the Second for the First, the Bond of the Trinity, is given to us to be one with our spirit. With this the way is open for us again to fully regain the likeness. And this is the whole challenge of life for us, to come to true unity of spirit with the Spirit, to once again be love, one with the Divine Love in the Being of God who is Love.

So far as we know, in the whole of the creation, with its fifteen billion galaxies fifteen billion years in evolution, we humans are the only creatures who can transform the Divine Creative Energies within us into Divine Love, into the fullness of freely chosen human communion, into personal communion and union with the Divine. Great visionaries through the centuries have pointed the way with ever greater clarity: the Rishis, Lao Tzu, Buddha, Confucius, Abraham and Moses, ultimately the incarnate God, Christ Jesus, whose revelation continues to unfold. In our own days we have seen it moving ahead, usually in its initial unleashing passing through a stage of chaos, in persons like Gandhi, Martin Luther King, Rosa Parks, Mother Teresa of Calcutta.

When we go to the center of our being and pass through that center into the very center of God, we get in immediate touch with this Divine Creating Energy. This is not a new idea. It is the common teaching of the Christian fathers of the Greek tradition. When we dare with the full assent of love to unleash these energies within us, not surprisingly the initial experience is of a flood of chaotic thoughts, memories, emotions, and feelings. This is why wise spiritual fathers and mothers counsel a gentle entering into this experience. Not too much too fast. But it is this release that allows all of this chaos within us with all its imprisoning stress to be brought into harmony so that not only there might be peace and harmony within but that the Divine Energy may have the freedom to forward the evolution of consciousness in us and through us, as a part of the whole, in the whole of the creation.

APPENDIX A

Centering Prayer

Sit relaxed and quiet.

1. Be in faith and love to God who dwells in the center of your being.

2. Take up a love word and let it be gently present, supporting your being to God in faith-filled love.

3. Whenever you become aware of anything, simply, gently return to the Lord with the use of your prayer word.

After twenty minutes let the Our Father (or some other prayer) pray itself.

APPENDIX B

The Method of Lectio

It is well to keep the Sacred Scriptures enthroned in our homes in a place of honor as a Real Presence of the Word in our midst.

1. We take the Sacred Text with reverence and call upon Holy Spirit.

2. For five minutes (longer, if we are so drawn) we listen to the Lord speaking to us through the Text and respond.

3. At the end of the time, we choose a word or phrase (perhaps one will have been "given" to us) to take with us and thank the Lord for being with us and speaking to us.

More briefly we might put it this way:

1. Come into the Presence and call upon Holy Spirit.

2. Listen for five minutes.

3. Thank the Lord and take a "word."

Some Helpful Reading

Bernard of Clairvaux. *The Works of Bernard of Clairvaux.* Trans. Michael Casey et al. Spencer, Mass., and Kalamazoo, Mich.: Cistercian Publications, 1969.

Chu-Cong, Joseph. *The Contemplative Experience.* New York: Crossroad, 1999.

Horney, Karen. *Neurosis and Human Growth.* New York: Norton, 1991.

Keating, Thomas. *Open Mind, Open Heart.* Warwick, N.Y.: Amity House, 1986.

————. *Reawakenings.* New York: Crossroad, 1992.

————. *Invitation to Love.* New York: Crossroad, 1993.

————. *Intimacy with God.* New York: Crossroad, 1994.

Keyes, Ken. *Handbook to Higher Consciousness.* Coos Bay, Ore.: Love Line Books, 1975.

May, Gerald. *Addiction and Grace: Love and Spirituality in the Healing of Addictions.* San Francisco: Harper, 1961.

——. *Will and Spirit: A Contemplative Psychology.* San Francisco: Harper, 1982.

McGinn, Bernard. *The Growth of Mysticism: Gregory the Great through the Twelfth Century.* New York: Crossroad, 1994.

Merton, Thomas. *The New Man.* New York: Farrar, Straus and Giroux, 1961.

——. *New Seeds of Contemplation.* New York: New Directions, 1961.

——. *The Climate of Monastic Prayer.* Spencer, Mass.: Cistercian Publications, 1969.

——. *Contemplation in a World of Action.* New York: Doubleday, 1971.

——. *Six Letters.* With Boris Pasternak. Lexington, Ky.: King Library Press, 1973.

——. *A Search for Solitude: The Journals of Thomas Merton: Volume Three, 1952–1960.* Ed. Lawrence S. Cunningham. San Francisco: HarperCollins, 1996.

Pennington, M. Basil. *Centering Prayer: Renewing an Ancient Christian Prayer Form.* New York: Doubleday, 1980.

————. *Call to the Center.* New York: Doubleday, 1990; Hyde Park, N.Y.: New City Press, 1995.

————. *Thomas Merton Brother Monk.* New York: Continuum, 1997.

————. *Lectio Divina: Renewing the Ancient Practice of Praying the Scriptures.* New York: Crossroad, 1998.

————. *Centered Living.* Liguori, Mo.: Liguori, 1999.

Piaget, Jean, and Barbel Inhelder. *The Psychology of the Child.* New York: Basic Books, 1969.

Reininger, Gustave, ed. *Centering Prayer in Daily Life and Ministry.* New York: Continuum, 1998.

————. *The Diversity of Centering Prayer.* New York: Continuum, 1999.

Toolan, David S. "Praying in a Post-Einsteinian Universe," *Cross Currents* 46 (1997): 437–70.

Wilber, Ken. *Up from Eden: A Transpersonal View of Human Evolution.* Wheaton, Ill.: Quest, 1996.

William of St.Thierry. *The Works of William of St.Thierry.* Trans. Penelope Lawson et al. Spencer, Mass., and Kalamazoo, Mich.: Cistercian Publications, 1969.